2

LOUISA MAY
ALCOTT

AMERICAN WOMEN of ACHIEVEMENT

LOUISA MAY ALCOTT

KATHLEEN BURKE

CHELSEA HOUSE PUBLISHERS

NEW YORK • PHILADELPHIA

Editor-in-Chief: Nancy Toff
Executive Editor: Remmel T. Nunn
Managing Editor: Karyn Gullen Browne
Copy Chief: Juliann Barbato
Picture Editor: Adrian G. Allen
Art Director: Giannella Garrett
Manufacturing Manager: Gerald Levine

Staff for LOUISA MAY ALCOTT:

Senior Editor: Constance Jones
Copyeditor: Terrance Dolan
Editorial Assistant: Theodore Keyes
Picture Researcher: Toby Greenberg
Designer: Design Oasis
Production Coordinator: Joseph Romano
Cover Illustration: Amanda Wilson

Creative Director: Harold Steinberg

3   5   7   9   8   6   4

Library of Congress Cataloging in Publication Data

Burke, Kathleen. LOUISA MAY ALCOTT.

(American women of achievement)
Bibliography: p.
Includes index.
1. Alcott, Louisa May, 1832–1888—Biography—Juvenile
literature.   2. Authors, American—19th century—Biography—
Juvenile literature.   [1. Alcott, Louisa May, 1832–1888.
2. Authors, American]   I. Title.   II. Series.
PS1018.B87   1988   813'.4 [B] [92]   87-21846

ISBN 1-55546-637-0
      0-7910-0407-4 (pbk.)

CONTENTS

AMERICAN WOMEN of ACHIEVEMENT

Abigail Adams
women's rights advocate

Jane Addams
social worker

Louisa May Alcott
author

Marian Anderson
singer

Susan B. Anthony
woman suffragist

Ethel Barrymore
actress

Clara Barton
*founder of the American
Red Cross*

Elizabeth Blackwell
physician

Nellie Bly
journalist

Margaret Bourke-White
photographer

Pearl Buck
author

Rachel Carson
biologist and author

Mary Cassatt
artist

Agnes De Mille
choreographer

Emily Dickinson
poet

Isadora Duncan
dancer

Amelia Earhart
aviator

Mary Baker Eddy
*founder of the Christian
Science church*

Betty Friedan
feminist

Althea Gibson
tennis champion

Emma Goldman
political activist

Helen Hayes
actress

Lillian Hellman
playwright

Katharine Hepburn
actress

Karen Horney
psychoanalyst

Anne Hutchinson
religious leader

Mahalia Jackson
gospel singer

Helen Keller
humanitarian

Jeane Kirkpatrick
diplomat

Emma Lazarus
poet

Clare Boothe Luce
author and diplomat

Barbara McClintock
biologist

Margaret Mead
anthropologist

Edna St. Vincent Millay
poet

Julia Morgan
architect

Grandma Moses
painter

Louise Nevelson
sculptor

Sandra Day O'Connor
Supreme Court justice

Georgia O'Keeffe
painter

Eleanor Roosevelt
diplomat and humanitarian

Wilma Rudolph
champion athlete

Florence Sabin
medical researcher

Beverly Sills
opera singer

Gertrude Stein
author

Gloria Steinem
feminist

Harriet Beecher Stowe
author and abolitionist

Mae West
entertainer

Edith Wharton
author

Phillis Wheatley
poet

Babe Didrikson Zaharias
champion athlete

CHELSEA HOUSE PUBLISHERS

"Remember the Ladies"

MATINA S. HORNER

Remember the Ladies." That is what Abigail Adams wrote to her husband John, then a delegate to the Continental Congress, as the Founding Fathers met in Philadelphia to form a new nation in March of 1776. "Be more generous and favorable to them than your ancestors. Do not put such unlimited power in the hands of the Husbands. If particular care and attention is not paid to the Ladies," Abigail Adams warned, "we are determined to foment a Rebellion, and will not hold ourselves bound by any Laws in which we have no voice, or Representation."

The words of Abigail Adams, one of the earliest American advocates of women's rights, were prophetic. Because when we have not "remembered the ladies," they have, by their words and deeds, reminded us so forcefully of the omission that we cannot fail to remember them. For the history of American women is as interesting and varied as the history of our nation as a whole. American women have played an integral part in founding, settling, and building our country. Some we remember as remarkable women who— against great odds—achieved distinction in the public arena: Anne Hutchinson, who in the 17th century became a charismatic religious leader; Phillis Wheatley, an 18th-century black slave who became a poet; Susan B. Anthony, whose name is synonymous with the 19th-century women's rights movement, and who led the struggle to enfranchise women; and, in our own century, Amelia Earhart, the first woman to cross the Atlantic Ocean by air.

7

These extraordinary women certainly merit our admiration, but other women, "common women," many of them all but forgotten, should also be recognized for their contributions to American thought and culture. Women have been community builders; they have founded schools and formed voluntary associations to help those in need; they have assumed the major responsibility for rearing children, passing on from one generation to the next the values that keep a culture alive. These and innumerable other contributions, once ignored, are now being recognized by scholars, students, and the public. It is exciting and gratifying to realize that a part of our history that was hardly acknowledged a few generations ago is now being studied and brought to light.

In recent decades, the field of women's history has grown from obscurity to a politically controversial splinter movement to academic respectability, in many cases mainstreamed into such traditional disciplines as history, economics, and psychology. Scholars of women, both female and male, have organized research centers at such prestigious institutions as Wellesley College, Stanford University, and the University of California. Other notable centers for women's studies are the Center for the American Woman and Politics at the Eagleton Institute of Politics at Rutgers University, the Henry A. Murray Research Center for the Study of Lives, at Radcliffe College, and the Women's Research and Education Institute, the research arm of the Congressional Caucus on Women's Issues. Other scholars and public figures have established archives and libraries, such as the Schlesinger Library on the History of Women in America, at Radcliffe College, and the Sophia Smith Collection, at Smith College, to collect and preserve the written and tangible legacies of women.

From the initial donation of the Women's Rights Collection in 1943, the Schlesinger Library grew to encompass vast collections documenting the manifold accomplishments of American women. Simultaneously, the women's movement in general and the academic discipline of women's studies in particular also began with a narrow definition and gradually expanded their mandate. Early causes such as woman suffrage and social reform, abolition and organized labor were joined by newer concerns such as the history of women in business and the professions and in politics and government; the study of the family; and social issues such as health policy and education.

Women, as historian Arthur M. Schlesinger, jr., once pointed out, "have constituted the most spectacular casualty of traditional history. They have made up at least half the human race, but you could never tell that by looking at the books historians write." The new breed of historians is remedying that omission. They have written books about immigrant women and about working-class women who struggled for survival in cities and about black women who met the challenges of life in rural areas. They are telling the stories of women who, despite the barriers of tradition and economics, became lawyers and doctors and public figures.

The women's studies movement has also led scholars to question traditional interpretations of their respective disciplines. For example, the study of war has traditionally been an exercise in military and political analysis, an examination of strategies planned and executed by men. But scholars of women's history have pointed out that wars have also been periods of tremendous change and even opportunity for women, because the very absence of men on the home front enabled them to expand their educational, economic, and professional activities and to assume leadership in their homes.

The early scholars of women's history showed a unique brand of courage in choosing to investigate new subjects and take new approaches to old ones. Often, like their subjects, they endured criticism and even ostracism by their academic colleagues. But their efforts have unquestionably been worthwhile, because with the publication of each new study and book another piece of the historical patchwork is sewn into place, revealing an increasingly comprehensive picture of the role of women in our rich and varied history.

Such books on groups of women are essential, but books that focus on the lives of individuals are equally indispensable. Biographies can be inspirational, offering their readers the example of people with vision who have looked outside themselves for their goals and have often struggled against great obstacles to achieve them. Marian Anderson, for instance, had to overcome racial bigotry in order to perfect her art and perform as a concert singer. Isadora Duncan defied the rules of classical dance to find true artistic freedom. Jane Addams had to break down society's notions of the proper role for women in order to create new social institutions, notably the settlement house. All of these women had to come to terms both with themselves and with the world in which they lived. Only then could they move ahead as pioneers in their chosen callings.

Biography can inspire not only by adulation but also by realism. It helps us to see not only the qualities in others that we hope to emulate, but also, perhaps, the weaknesses that made them "human." By helping us identify with the subject on a more personal level they help us to feel that we, too, can achieve such goals. We read about Eleanor Roosevelt, for instance, who occupied a unique and seemingly enviable position as the wife of the president. Yet we can sympathize with her inner dilemma: an inherently shy woman, she had to force herself to live a most public life in order to use her position to benefit others. We may not be able to imagine ourselves having the immense poetic talent of Emily Dickinson, but from her story we can understand the challenges faced by a creative woman who was expected to fulfill many family responsibilities. And though few of us will ever reach the level of athletic accomplishment displayed by Wilma Rudolph or Babe Zaharias, we can still appreciate their spirit, their overwhelming will to excel.

A biography is a multifaceted lens. It is first of all a magnification, the intimate examination of one particular life. But at the same time, it is a wide-angle lens, informing us about the world in which the subject lived. We come away from reading about one life knowing more about the social, political, and economic fabric of the time. It is for this reason, perhaps, that the great New England essayist Ralph Waldo Emerson wrote, in 1841, "There is properly no history: only biography." And it is also why biography, and particularly women's biography, will continue to fascinate writers and readers alike.

LOUISA MAY
ALCOTT

Louisa May Alcott, as a child and later as a young woman, displayed little interest in the things most girls were concerned with. Behind her intense eyes and earnest expression were thoughts of fame and independence.

ONE

Miles from Home

Late on a December afternoon in 1862, as the sun faded from the wintry sky, a young woman bundled in a brown greatcoat and wearing a black bonnet strode briskly toward Concord village's train station. Encumbered by two portmanteaus and a basket of provisions, she arrived just in time to jostle aboard a train bound for Boston and Washington, D.C. In ways she could not begin to imagine, the journey would change her life.

After 3 days' travel, Louisa May Alcott, 30-year-old daughter of Bronson and Abba Alcott, would report for duty as a Civil War nurse. The conflict between the North and the South was raging in all its early savagery; in the overcrowded hospitals, women were desperately needed to tend the flow of casualties. The battle of Fredericks-burg alone—fought in Virginia just 50 miles south of Washington—would soon claim 12,600 Union and 5,300 Confederate lives.

As she watched the familiar Massachusetts landscape slip past her window, Alcott's head was filled with memories of home. For all her courage in facing the challenge ahead, she found herself blinking back tears. Even as a grown woman, she had rarely been separated from the household in which she had grown up. Her parents—(Amos) Bronson Alcott, the dreamer, educational reformer, and passionate intellectual; and Abigail ("Abba") May, wise and kind, resourceful and energetic—bred of old New England stock—had raised four daughters. Louisa was the second oldest.

Those extraordinary Alcotts would, of course, one day come to life in Louisa's autobiographical novel, *Little Women*, her portrait of a Victorian family. The book would sell 38,000 copies in 1869, the year it appeared, and would establish Alcott as one of the most celebrated authors of her day. In the character of Jo March—impetuous, sharp-tongued, imaginative, and compassionate—Alcott would draw on her own adolescence to create a complex, unforgettable heroine.

Yet *Little Women* and fame lay in the future as Alcott made the journey to Washington. As the train rumbled along in the dark, she lay awake smoothing her thick chestnut hair back from her face, hoping she could summon the strength for what lay before her. Stories of the soldiers' sufferings had already begun to reach the North. During her long night's journey, Alcott vowed to bring every ounce of her energy to the men carried in from the front.

Bronson Alcott had taught his daughters, from earliest childhood, that for people to own other people was a terrible wrong. Louisa May Alcott was determined to tend those

The Battle of Fredericksburg, fought just within the borders of Confederate Virginia, was one of the fiercest early clashes between Union and Confederate soldiers. All told, 17,900 men died on the field.

soldiers fighting slavery on the battle-fields. "Help needed, and I love nurs-ing, and must let out my pent-up energy in some new way," she con-fided to her journal.

To her task she brought even more than her courage and her lively sense of humor: Alcott came to her experi-ence with a writer's eye. By the early 1860s, she had published a number of what she called "sensational stories"— romances and melodramas— that sold well. Her thrillers, hastily penned and published under the pseudonym A. M. Barnard, helped support the Alcotts— who, it seemed, were always living on the brink of poverty. Bronson, regarded as one of the most brilliant philosoph-ical thinkers of the time, simply could not shackle himself to steady work.

During her six weeks as a soldiers' nurse at the makeshift Union Hotel Hospital just outside Washington in Georgetown, Alcott used her keen powers of observation to note and store away every detail of her experi-ence. She recounted her experiences in a book published under her own name in August 1863. With the appear-ance of *Hospital Sketches*, favorably reviewed across the nation, her career as a professional writer—during which she would publish some 270 works— truly began. Even today, Alcott's ac-count of Civil War suffering is as vivid and moving as if her readers had sat at her side in the fetid wards.

"I never began the year in a stranger place than this," wrote Alcott to her family early in 1863, "five hundred miles from home, alone, among strang-ers, doing painful duties all day long, leading a life of constant excitement in this great house, surrounded by three or four hundred men in all stages of suffering, disease, and death. Though often homesick, heartsick and worn out, I like it, find real pleasure in comforting, tending, and cheering these poor souls who seem to love me, to feel my sympathy though unspoken, and acknowledge my hearty good-will, in spite of the ignorance, awkward-ness, and bashfulness which I cannot help showing in so new and trying a situation."

The conditions she discovered in the hospital were nothing short of appalling. The dilapidated hotel, hast-ily converted to a hospital, was a maze of narrow hallways, peeling wallpaper, and often dank and airless rooms. "A more perfect pestilence-box than this house I never saw," observed Alcott, "cold, damp, dirty, full of vile odors from wounds, kitchens, wash-rooms and stables." And, in addition to the frightful conditions, she found "no competent head, male or female, to right matters, and a jumble of good, bad, and indifferent nurses, surgeons, and attendants, to complete the chaos still more."

Although her descriptions of the

Alcott spent six weeks as a volunteer nurse at the overcrowded Union Hotel Hospital in Georgetown before eventually succumbing to a severe case of typhoid. She never completely regained her health.

hospital's squalid quarters left an indelible impression on readers of her sketches, it was Louisa's portraits of the men themselves that families, gathered around kitchen tables and hearthsides across the country, read again and again. To many of them, it seemed they could see their own brother, husband, or son in Alcott's patients. Three days after her arrival in Washington, the soldiers wounded at Fredericksburg—a crushing defeat for the Union army—began filling the hospital to overflowing. Their arrival was a sight that haunted her for the rest of her life: "In they came, some on stretchers, some in men's arms, some staggering along propped on rude crutches . . . ragged, gaunt, and pale, mud to the knees, with bloody bandages untouched since put on days before; many bundled up in blankets, coats being lost or useless; and all wearing that disheartened look which proclaimed defeat."

In the wards, where men lay in beds pushed one against the other, Alcott discovered subject after subject for her profiles in courage. A young sergeant with one leg gone, and an arm about to be amputated, greeted her cheerfully enough: "Now don't you fret yourself about me, Miss, I'm first rate here, for it's nuts to lie still on this bed, knocking about in those confounded ambulances, that shake what there is left of a fellow to jelly." As for Judgment Day, he added wryly, he might encounter some difficulties: "My leg will have to tramp from Fredericksburg, my arm from here, I suppose, and meet my body, wherever it may be." At this thought, her patient, Alcott reported, "laughed blithely." Nurse Alcott, who always managed to find what little merriment there was in that house of suffering, joined him.

Filled with respect for the men she nursed, Alcott worked tirelessly in the wards. But as the weeks of hard work, emotional strain, and insufficient rest passed, Alcott's energy flagged. Then one day she awoke feeling ill. Unwilling to leave her patients and sure that hers was only a minor ailment, Alcott reported to her post. When she arrived at the hospital, however, she collapsed.

Orderlies carried her to bed; through a blur of delirium, Alcott recognized nurses and doctors peering at her anxiously. "Dream awfully, and wake unrefreshed, think of home, and wonder if I am to die here," she recorded in her journal on January 4. Alcott had contracted typhoid fever, like many other nurses who became ill. Exposed to diseases—cholera, pneumonia, scarlet fever—carried by the troops, Civil War nurses often died. Alcott's case was very grave: On January 16 Bronson Alcott arrived to bring his daughter back to Concord. Louisa, delerious, was barely conscious of her leave-taking: "Quite a flock came to see me off," she recalled later, "but I was too sick to have but a dim idea of what was going on."

For three weeks, as she hovered on the brink of death, the family nursed her. Bronson and Abba and May, the youngest of Alcott's sisters, took turns waiting at her side. Anna, her eldest sister, visited as often as she could leave her husband behind and make the journey from Boston. Although Anna was expecting a baby soon, she often sat in her sister's sickroom, waiting and hoping for her recovery.

At last, Alcott regained consciousness. Her nightmarish hallucinations and her visions of suffering men diminished. She scarcely recognized herself: A gaunt, angular, and sallow face stared back in the mirror, and she had lost most of her luxuriant hair. "Didn't know myself at all," she announced.

Hospital Sketches stands as a startlingly vivid memorial to the tragedy of the Civil War. Alcott's moving descriptions of wounded and dying soldiers were read throughout the nation.

Anna, the oldest of the Alcott sisters, was the first to marry. Upon her husband's death, however, she returned home and helped Louisa Alcott take care of their father.

"When I tried to walk, I couldn't, and cried because my legs wouldn't go."

Hers was a long and painful convalescence. The recovery proved all the more difficult because the hospital physicians had treated her with calomel, a commonly prescribed 19th-century purgative drug believed to purify the system. But the drug contains mercury, and it seriously damaged Alcott's health. For the rest of her life she would suffer headaches, insomnia, and muscle tremors. "I was never ill before," she wrote of that period, "and never well after."

Not until the spring did Alcott regain her strength or feel well enough to sit at her desk and work. From that room on the second floor of Orchard House, the family home, she looked out from two south-facing windows upon Concord's frame houses and neat grid of streets. The village was, for the writer, a state of mind as well as a place. Her father's circle of intellectual companions, including the philosopher Ralph Waldo Emerson and the writer Henry Thoreau, had taught young Louisa to thrive on a life of ideas. Surrounded by her favorite books and prints, she began writing steadily, giving voice and shape to her memories of the Union Hotel Hospital.

In May, *Hospital Sketches* appeared as a four-part series in *Commonwealth*, a journal published by reformers who advocated that slavery be abolished.

Ralph Waldo Emerson, American essayist and poet, was a member of Bronson Alcott's intellectual circle. Surrounded by men of letters as a child, it was only natural for Louisa Alcott to turn to writing as an adult.

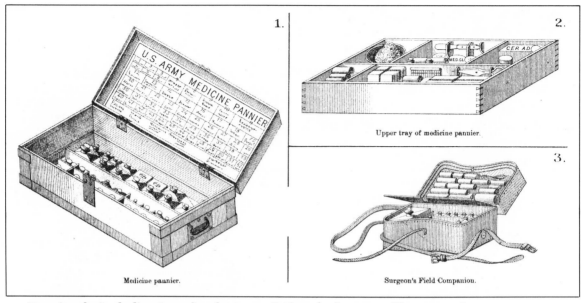

1.

U.S. ARMY MEDICINE PANNIER

2.

Upper tray of medicine pannier.

3.

Medicine pannier.

Surgeon's Field Companion.

Despite their dedication, the doctors of Alcott's day were ill prepared to treat battlefield wounds. As often as not, a soldier was successfully treated for injuries only to die of one of the many diseases prevalent in the wards.

Magazines across the country then reprinted the pieces. From every corner, reviewers praised Alcott's "graphically drawn" scenes as "fluent and sparkling with touches of quiet humor." By August, the first copies of *Sketches*, bound in green covers, arrived at Orchard House. Before long, letters poured into the Concord post office. Scores of correspondents wrote to tell Alcott of their admiration for her simple, eloquent accounts of the men she had served faithfully and well.

As if the months of idleness had filled her with ideas, Alcott produced an enormous variety of stories. Under the pseudonym A. M. Barnard, she continued to write the romantic thrillers that commanded gratifying profits. She frequently traveled to Washington Street, Boston's "literary row," to deliver manuscripts—sometimes as "Miss Barnard" and sometimes, with her other, more serious efforts, as "L. M. Alcott."

Her first real success, *Hospital Sketches*, was a heartening antidote to the months of illness and delirium. Alcott exulted in the recognition the book had earned her: "If there ever was an astonished young woman, it is I myself," she wrote, "for things have gone so swimmingly I don't know who I am. A year ago I had no publisher;

now three have asked me for something [and] several papers are ready to print my contributions.... There is a sudden hoist for a meek and lowly scribbler!" In the wake of this good fortune, she worked hard on her first adult novel, *Moods*. The book, praised by many reviewers, appeared in the autumn of 1864.

As much as she enjoyed exercising the powers of her own creativity, Alcott never forgot that, for her, writing was a way of making a livelihood for her family. Bronson Alcott had just lost another of the jobs—this time as Concord school superintendent—that he was never able to hold down. It was up to his daughter to "pay all the debts, fix the house . . . and keep the old folks cosey." Alcott's generosity of heart never failed in the face of her family's needs. "I . . . devote time & earnings to my father and mother," she wrote, "for one possesses no gift for money making & the other is now too old to work any longer for those who are happy & able to work for her."

As 1863 ended and she reviewed her accounts, Alcott noted that of her earnings—"from writing alone"—she had spent very little on herself. This was to be true throughout her life: Anxious as she was for everyone's welfare, she rarely indulged her own wishes and rarely looked after her own happiness.

Henry David Thoreau, one of America's most revered authors, was never too busy to spend time with the Alcott children. Louisa Alcott in particular thrived under his liberal tutelage.

As a writer, she enjoyed her first triumph—soon she would be recognized as a national celebrity. As a dutiful daughter, she cared for her parents. As a steadfast sister, she prepared to send May, an aspiring artist, off to study in Italy. Perhaps, though, she did not yet allow herself to dream her own dreams as fully as she might.

An elderly Bronson Alcott sits on the steps of the chapel that doubled as his lecture room in Concord, where the educator found a more receptive audience for his unorthodox teaching methods and philosophy than he had in Boston.

TWO

The Road to Concord

"She is a very fine . . . little creature," reported Bronson Alcott of his second daughter, christened Louisa May and born on her father's birthday, November 29, 1832. Straightaway he noted that the baby differed distinctly from her two-year-old sister: She was "much larger than Anna at birth," he observed, "with a fine constitution for building up a fine character." Anna was placid and sunny from her earliest day. She was her father's daughter: blond and blue-eyed as were all the Alcott clan. Louisa, on the other hand, proved bold, adventurous, and stubborn from the start. Her chestnut hair and brown eyes—and her temper and high spirits—marked her, through and through, as one of the Mays, her mother's family.

Abba Alcott, like her daughter, was fiery and strong willed. She had grown up in a large, lively, and prosperous Boston family, the youngest daughter of a distinguished civic leader and philanthropist. On her mother's side, she was related to a number of eminent Bostonians. Because of her privileged background, she sometimes found life as a young wife and mother trying; living with her husband and two small daughters near Philadelphia, she faced a daunting array of household and child-care chores. Bronson Alcott's salary as a schoolmaster did not allow for domestic help, and he worked long hours at his teaching. When he was at home, he gave over many hours to writing and studying.

Even so, Abba Alcott willingly shouldered her responsibilities. She took enormous pride in her husband's ac-

Abigail May ("Abba") Alcott was descended from a prosperous and highly respected Boston family, but she managed to adjust to life with an impractical, though beloved, husband who made little income.

an imaginative teacher could do. The tall, lanky young man with a finely chiseled face carted more than 100 books into his classroom, as well as flowers and pine boughs to brighten the bleak interior, and arranged that each child should have a desk. He taught geography by asking the students to draw a map of their own schoolyard, arithmetic by adding and subtracting with beans and blocks of wood rather than scrawling out the sums on a chalkboard—he even introduced gymnastics!

Bronson Alcott came to Philadelphia at the request of some Quaker families who had heard of his talents. They wanted their own children to experience his gentle and generous approach to learning. The teacher, for his part, admired the Quakers' concern for the lot of their fellow humans. Later, in the days when the Alcotts had barely enough to eat, they always shared the little they had with anyone in need.

As involved as they were in the life of Germantown, a pleasant rural area on the outskirts of Philadelphia, the Alcotts missed Boston and longed to return there. When the most important backer of Bronson Alcott's school, a Quaker merchant, died suddenly, the family decided to return to Massachusetts.

They arrived on July 10, 1834, with only a few possessions—they had sold nearly all their worldly goods to pay

complishments, for he was conducting an important experiment in his classroom. His view—virtually unheard of in those days of cold and cheerless schoolhouses and stern-faced taskmasters—was that children should enjoy learning.

At his first assignment, in Cheshire, Connecticut, Alcott had shown what debts. Soon Alcott had established what was to become his most famous experiment, the Temple School, where he continued his innovative efforts to stimulate original thinking and self-expression in his young students. Abba Alcott tended her two older daughters and looked after a new arrival—blue-eyed, brown-haired Lizzie, a tranquil infant born within that first year in Boston. In the 1830s, Boston was a city to delight the eye: Redbrick row houses lined the cobbled streets, tall-masted ships sailed into the crowded harbor, sturdy trees graced the green common set at the city's heart, and Thomas Bullfinch's elegant, gold-domed state-house was rising in all its splendor.

For young Louisa, Boston was a tantalizing world to be explored; every byway seemed to beckon her. One day the temptation proved irresistible for the adventurous six-year-old. Louisa walked and walked, mesmerized by

A traditional Quaker meeting. Bronson Alcott taught Quaker children in Philadelphia before returning to Boston to establish the Temple School. The Quakers' mild ways and concern for others made a lasting impression on the Alcotts.

Boston's Quincy Market teemed with activity in the 19th century. Ships from around the world provided exotic goods for the city's prosperous citizens.

the life of the city. By afternoon, she had reached the wharf, where men carried crates of oranges, rum, and exotic spices. Absorbed in the sights, she had become completely lost. Resting in the doorway of a row house, she fell asleep against a large shaggy Newfoundland dog. When she woke to hear the town crier calling: "Lost! One little girl with curly brown hair, a white frock, and green shoes," Louisa sang out, "Here I am!" and rode home on his shoulder. Her parents were too

relieved to scold her harshly—but they could only wonder where Louisa's curiosity would take her next.

There was only one place in Boston she found more alluring than the busy streets and gracious common: her father's school. Located on the top floor of the redbrick Masonic Temple town house, Alcott's classroom was filled with interesting objects. Light poured in upon the rich carpets; the chairs were arranged in a semicircle around the teacher's desk; and slates, books,

City Hall, Boston. As a child, Alcott loved the hustle and bustle of Boston, but in adolescence she developed a deep love for the country and its less hurried ways.

busts of famous philosophers, globes, and blocks filled the room. Here the teacher and his students had lively discussions instead of engaging in meaningless repetitions of "common-places" (passages memorized from books), which prevailed in the more traditional classrooms. Louisa, from the time she was three, had longed to sit with the students as her older sister Anna did—but she had to wait until she turned four.

Bronson Alcott's heart was, above all, bound up with books. Louisa shared this passion—sometimes building great towers of her father's dictionaries, always listening at his side as he read stories. All his life, her father had difficulty looking beyond his study. When his students' parents began questioning Alcott's unorthodox teaching methods, wondering why their children weren't reeling off the same facts and figures recited by other boys and girls, he grew resentful and disappointed. One by one, families be-

An attentive audience looks on as Bronson Alcott gives a lecture at the School of Philosophy in the chapel at Concord. His friends Emerson and the Thoreau brothers were the school's original founders.

gan removing children. The loss of each student meant a decrease in Alcott's salary. Soon the Alcotts were—for the first of many times—living on the edge of poverty.

A solution came in the form of a helping hand from Ralph Waldo Emerson, one of America's most influential authors and thinkers. Emerson and Bronson Alcott became fast friends after the scholar from Concord visited Alcott's school. Emerson was also a man interested in ideas—in progressive education, in freeing black slaves, in the strength and courage of the individual, in the expanding frontier of America. His unique vision was one of the forces behind American transcendentalism, an idealistic philosophical and literary movement whose members believed in the divinity of man and nature and emphasized self-reliance, individualism, and the rejection of authority. As one who spent long hours in his study reading, thinking, and writing, he understood that Bronson Alcott needed a place where he could live the life of his mind.

Emerson's School of Philosophy gave lecturers the chance to air their theories before interested citizens and students. His own philosophy of American Transcendentalism was to attract many followers.

Emerson arranged for the family to settle in his home village, Concord, 20 miles west of central Boston. As the family bundled their belongings into a coach for the three-hour journey in April 1840, Abba Alcott noticed that Louisa had taken out a notebook and was recording every detail of their departure from the city. At age seven, she was already an avid writer.

Emerson rented the Alcotts a small brown-frame cottage, set in a garden, near the Concord River. Bronson Alcott shelved his books in neat rows in his study and rolled up his sleeves to dig a vegetable plot. His wife, delighted at the fine prospect of field and river, went about singing in the kitchen. And Louisa discovered the exhilarating freedom of the countryside: "I always

thought," she said later, "I must have been a deer or a horse in some former state, because it was such a joy to run. Nobody could be my friend 'til I had beaten him in a race, and no girl if she refused to climb fences, and be a tomboy."

Even more liberating than Concord's open spaces was the classroom Louisa found there. Until this time, Louisa

To Louisa
1839

My Daughter,

You are Seven years old to day, and your Father is forty. You have learned a great many things, since you have lived in a Body, about things going on around you, and within you. You know how to think, how to resolve, how to love, and how to obey. You feel your Conscience, and have no real pleasure unless you obey it.

Throughout her life, Alcott had a close relationship with her father, whose involvement in the Transcendentalist movement profoundly influenced her. Pictured is an excerpt from a letter he wrote to her on her seventh birthday, which was his fortieth.

Threatened by imminent poverty in Boston, the Alcotts accepted Emerson's invitation to live in the rural community of Concord. There, Bronson Alcott dedicated himself to intellectual pursuits, and his children had the whole outdoors for a classroom.

Thoreau, in one slender volume, immortalized the isolated body of water known as Walden Pond. In Walden, he recorded a philosophy of humanity's place in nature, which he had developed during his two-year stay at the pond.

and Anna had studied under their father. Now Bronson allowed them to attend a school organized by Henry David Thoreau, a young Harvard graduate and Emerson's friend. Thoreau and his brother John approached education in the same spirit as did Alcott. They explored ideas alongside the children, but even more importantly, they introduced the outdoors as a classroom.

For Louisa, who loved the forest and field and every living creature, her excursions with Thoreau were never to be forgotten. A short, stocky man with a craggy face, piercing blue eyes, and a kindly smile, Thoreau knew every inch of Concord's woodlands. He took the children hiking mile after mile, stopping to point out the names of wildflowers, the flash of a scarlet tanager so bright that it "seemed to set the forest on fire," the secret glens where blue-berries grew. In his little skiff, painted green for the grass and blue for the sky, Thoreau rowed the children along pond and stream, looking at water lilies and searching out otters' dens on the banks. His love of nature would later become known throughout the world in his classic book, *Walden*, a record of his solitary two-year stay on Walden Pond near Concord.

Louisa thrived under Thoreau's teaching and under the succession of fair days and clear nights in Concord. During this period, she began writing in earnest, composing her own plays and creating her own productions of stories she had known and loved, including *Jack and the Beanstalk* and *Cinderella*. Louisa and the neighborhood children staged elaborate productions in a nearby barn—with Louisa Alcott as the writer, director, and often starring actress as well.

As Alcott approached young adulthood, she refused to conform to the restrictions society placed upon women. She never guessed that with her pen she would transcend even her own expectations of greatness.

THREE

Green Fields

For all of Concord's many pleasures, though, life in the Alcott household could seem as difficult as ever. Bronson Alcott found no employment there other than cutting wood for one dollar a day. He had given up the idea of teaching, convinced that he was destined to be misunderstood. The family subsisted on the contributions of kind neighbors (especially Emerson) and occasional loans from Abba May Alcott's family. And there was a new mouth to feed: sunny, dimpled May, who was born that first fair summer in Concord. Louisa was keenly aware of the hardships imposed on her mother, who struggled to keep her daughters fed and clothed. Her determination to save her mother from worry and want grew greater day by day. She had not even begun to dream that she could accomplish that with her pen.

Bronson Alcott's dreams of the simple life, of human fellowship and harmony, took his family on a strange new journey early in the summer of 1843. Alcott and several like-minded companions joined in a communal farming enterprise. They bought a rambling, spare farmhouse on a wooded hill 15 miles from Concord. It was an isolated, windswept spot with commanding views of the mountains. Alcott called the farmstead Fruitlands—reflecting his hope that he and his followers would reap rich harvests there.

At Fruitlands, Alcott practiced his conviction that life should be reduced to its most essential elements. The men planted most of their crops—

Although Alcott's parents enjoyed the quiet country atmosphere of Concord, they found it difficult to make a living there.

with farming and household chores, studied their lessons for hours, and sang hymns at day's end.

Louisa's diary from the early days at Fruitlands gives a glimpse of this period, when she was ten:

"September 1st. I rose at five and had my bath. I love cold water! Then we had our singing lesson. After breakfast I washed dishes, and ran on the hill till nine. . . . It was so beautiful up there. Did my lessons,—wrote and spelt and did sums. . . .

We had bread and fruit for dinner. I read and walked and played till supper-time. . . . As I went to bed the moon came up very brightly and looked at me. I felt sad because I have been cross today, and did not mind Mother. . . . I get to sleep saying poetry,—I know a great deal."

Over that summer, the settlers at Fruitlands had planted busily, then tended the crops, and, with hopes for the future, watched the succession of hot days and clear, cool nights. Still, as the autumn winds began to whistle through chinks in the walls and cracks in the windows, a cloud of gloom seemed to fall over the household. The harvest was somewhat meager; the store of vegetables and apples surely would not last through the winter. Abba Alcott complained that she had taken on the backbreaking household chores virtually by herself and, in protest, sometimes refused to take part in

barley, rye, and oats—by hand. Everyone shared a strictly vegetarian diet: porridge, bread, and water at breakfast; a lunch of bread, water, and vegetables; water, bread, and fruit in the evening. Warm water for bathing was not allowed. The Alcott daughters helped

May Alcott's birth, welcomed as it was, added to the Alcotts' financial distress. Though only 10 years old at the time, Louisa Alcott became determined to lighten her mother's burdens someday.

the meals she herself prepared. Louisa chafed under the routines of this experiment in community, especially at the long hours of lessons presided over by unfamiliar adults bent on instructing the young. In October, as the situation became more worrisome, she found herself writing: "I wish I was rich, I was good, and we were all a happy family this day."

The notion of "a happy family" seemed increasingly unattainable as winter approached. Bronson Alcott's disciples at Fruitlands were asking him to make a very difficult choice. The only way to lead an exemplary life, they felt, was to break the confining ties of family. On other nearby experimental farmsteads, women, men, and children lived in separate compounds. Alcott began to consider forming one of these groups.

The entire family discussed this possibility one evening in November. Louisa was heartsick at the idea of such a separation: "Father and Mother and Anna and I had a long talk. I was very unhappy, and we all cried. Anna and I cried in bed, and I prayed to God to keep us together."

Dark and fearful as the moment seemed, the family somehow did weather the crisis. For all his dreams of living in a new kind of fellowship, Bronson Alcott remained tied to his wife and children by strong affections. At last he acknowledged that the Fruit-

lands experiment had been a failure. There were neither provisions nor firewood to last the winter. Other members of the circle went off to join nearby communal farms. The Alcotts were, once again, a family to themselves.

Bronson Alcott emerged from Fruitlands bitter and disappointed. He withdrew more and more, often not moving from his room in their rented lodgings for days at a time, eating little more than apples and water. Abba Alcott was at her wits' end, weighed down by worries, when she received a small inheritance from her father's estate. She used the money to buy a rambling, tumbledown, but charming farmhouse in Concord. Set in a meadow near a pine forest, the new home was christened Hillside by the Alcotts. The snug, low-ceilinged farmhouse, with its porch and peaked gables, provided the setting for a period of happiness and serenity. The years Louisa spent there—from the spring she was 13 to the winter she turned 16—became the basis for the March household described in loving detail in *Little Women*.

Taking over Hillside seemed to return Bronson Alcott to his old energies. The scars of the Fruitlands failure seemed to heal as he set himself to the task of repairing the old house and restoring its gardens and grounds. He hammered and nailed and planted—

Fruitlands, the communal living project founded by Bronson Alcott and his transcendentalist associates in 1843, lasted only six months. The farmstead was one of several such experimental communities to spring up in response to the widespread 19th-century desire for a simpler life.

squash and lettuce, peas and beans, buckwheat and rye, turnips and beets, melons and corn—and weeded and pruned. He supervised the division of an old shed into two rooms, each of which were added as wings to the house. One wing served as his study, the other as a special room for Louisa.

41

The March family home in Little Women, illustrated above, was based upon Hillside, the Alcotts' beloved Concord farmhouse. The family spent three years at Hillside before financial problems forced them back to Boston.

Meg March packs her trunk for a journey. Just as Hillside served as a model for the March home, Alcott's own sisters were the prototypes for the March girls.

The March sisters. Her family's return to Boston proved very difficult for Alcott. Writing the story of the March family allowed her to relive the rural childhood she was forced to leave behind.

43

Throughout her life, Alcott cherished private retreats in which she could think and write. She enjoyed her first such sanctum at Hillside, and 25 years later set up her room at Orchard House (pictured), where she wrote Little Women.

She took possession proudly: Louisa had always dreamed of having a room of her own. "It does one good to be alone," she noted in her journal, "and Mother has made it very pretty and neat for me." Her desk sat under the window; her sewing basket at her side. The closet was fresh with the scent of dried herbs, and the door opened on to the garden so Louisa could "run off to the woods whenever I like." The room was, above all, a place for Louisa to sort out her thoughts and to write.

Writing was now becoming one of the defining passions of her life—from the small desk she poured out stories, poems, sketches, and plays.

Hillside also boasted a great, airy barn where the four sisters produced a series of Louisa's plays for an audience of friends and neighbors. Her creations, inevitably swashbuckling and romantic, bore titles such as "Norma, or the Witches' Curse," "A Captive of Castile," "The Unloved Wife," and "The Prince and the Peasant."

Hillside was also the place where Louisa struggled with her own ambitions and the changeable emotions of adolescence. She felt herself destined for some kind of greatness, vowing to accomplish wonderful things "by and by." "Don't care what," she mused, "teaching, sewing, acting, writing, anything to help the family, and I'll be rich and famous and happy before I die, see if I don't."

Louisa's dilemma was indeed difficult. Young women were expected to be docile and compliant and to serve the needs and dreams of others. In fact, until early in the 20th century, women were virtually regarded as the property of their husbands and were not permitted to own property, sign contracts, obtain credit, go into business, or control their own earnings. The law was structured to confine women to the home and family. Louisa could not help bridling at the restrictions and could not help noticing that a wider world opened itself to men and boys. She herself often lamented these limitations. "That she was not a boy was one of her great afflictions," a friend recalled many years later. "Her impulsive disposition was fretted by the restraints . . . which were deemed essential to the proper girl." Louisa was tall and strong, and said to be the fastest runner in her school. She wondered why she should not be allowed to aim as high or to race as hard as boys her age.

These questions—and the story ideas that seemed to swarm into her head night and day—often kept her awake late into the summer nights. When she could not sleep, she slipped out to the cherry orchard and climbed one of the gnarled trees. In the top branches, she thought her own thoughts and listened to her own imagination until the flutter of owls in the darkness made her scramble for the safety of her own room.

Weary immigrants wait on Ellis Island for the ferry that will take them to New York City. Immigrants came to Boston by the thousands as well, bringing with them new energy and skills, but also new problems.

FOUR

Out to Service

Serene as life at Hillside was, and important as it proved to Louisa's development as a writer, the interlude ended after little more than two years. Abba Alcott's meager inheritance could not sustain the family indefinitely, and the rambling old house began falling into disrepair. Friends from Boston offered Louisa's mother work that would engage all of her talents. She was known throughout Concord and beyond as an unfailingly resourceful woman. Whenever another family was in dire need, without warm clothing or food or firewood, Abba Alcott somehow would find a way to provide. Why, her friends asked, should she not bring her skills to Boston, where her abilities were much in demand?

The city to which Abba Alcott re-turned in 1849 had changed enormously. Since 1840, more than 50,000 Irish immigrants had flooded into Boston. They were, by and large, impoverished and uneducated tenant farmers, driven from their land by famine and greedy, heartless landlords. Crowded into tenements where as many as 15 persons might occupy one room, the Irish lived in a community where disease and despair flourished. Abba Alcott assumed her duties as an "assistant"—in fact, one of the first social workers—to the immigrants. She took on the work eagerly: "My heart has always been pledged to the cause of the destitute," she observed. "Now my time shall be sacredly devoted to their relief."

Abba Alcott found that all of her talents were called upon, and she was soon immersed in work that was exhausting but absorbing. Given her genius for management and her eloquence at reporting the conditions she investigated, she proved herself equal to the challenge. Yet for her daughter Louisa, the very horizon seemed to narrow as she returned to Boston. She had not wanted to leave Concord, and the idea of giving Hillside over to tenants had seemed almost unbearable.

Louisa remembered the move to Boston as a time when life seemed to close in on her: "I was left to keep house, feeling like a caged sea gull as I washed dishes and cooked in the basement kitchen, where my prospect was limited to a procession of muddy boots." Surrounded as she was by family, she found it difficult to express how wrenching the displacement had been. Her very imagination felt threatened by the city's "bustle and dirt and change," the confusion that "sends all lovely images and restful feelings away." "Among my hills and woods," she mourned, "I had fine free times alone. . . . I see now what Nature did for me, and my 'romantic tastes,' as people call that love of solitude and out-of-door life, taught me much. . . ." With no room of her own, she found it almost impossible to spin her dreams into stories.

Sixteen-year-old Louisa experienced her removal from Hillside as division between adolescence and young adulthood. Neither she nor her sisters could ignore the misery that they saw around them and that they experienced each evening as their mother described her day's encounters. "We were now beginning to play our parts on a real stage," Alcott wrote, "and to know something of the pathetic side of life, with its hard facts, irksome duties, many temptations and the daily sacrifice of self." She was introducing the theme of becoming "little women."

One of the "hard facts" that was inescapable for Anna, Louisa, Lizzie, and May Alcott was that they must help support the family. Their father kept to his scholarly projects and could not settle into any gainful employment. For the next two years, Alcott tried her hand at whatever she could find. In addition to overseeing the household, she tutored and cared for small children and sewed in an attempt to ease her family's situation. She and Anna organized a small school that brought them meager earnings.

At that moment, when Alcott described her family as "poor as rats and forgotten by everyone but the Lord," a lawyer from nearby Dedham came to Abba Alcott in search of household help. He sought a companion for the aged father and invalid sister who shared his household. The duties, he assured her, were to be "light," consisting largely of reading to the shut-ins.

A view of Milldam Road from the foot of Beacon Street in a prosperous district of Boston. Though Boston was known for its wealth and sophistication, by 1849 more than 50,000 Irish immigrants had poured into the city and lived in intolerably crowded and disease-ridden tenements.

When Abba Alcott asked her daughter Louisa whether she knew of anyone to take on the post, she replied, "Only myself." Although the gentleman stated merely that the salary would be "sufficient," surely, reasoned Alcott, she could earn more than by sewing and tutoring. So she packed herself off to Dedham for seven weeks—an experience she would later describe in the story "How I Went Out to Service" and in her novel *Work*.

The Dedham episode was, in fact, a grueling ordeal. Alcott found herself taking on hard labor of every description — carrying in great buckets of coal

LOUISA M. ALCOTT'S FAMOUS BOOKS

WORK:

A STORY OF EXPERIENCE.

"An endless significance lies in work; in idleness alone is there perpetual despair." — CARLYLE.

PRICE $1.50.

These books are sold by all booksellers and newsdealers everywhere. When not to be found, send the advertised amount by mail, to the Publishers,

ROBERTS BROTHERS, Boston

Alcott drew upon her own unhappy experience as a nurse for two invalids in writing her novel Work. *The first editor who read the manuscript rejected it out of hand.*

and hoisting buckets of well water up the steep stairs; shoveling snow from the walks, sweeping ashes, splitting wood, and tending fires; all the while waiting on two fretful and helpless invalids. Her visions of reading novels by the fire to brighten the days of her patients gave way to despair in that drafty, cheerless setting. All the while, her employer never mentioned payment for her services.

Although she had promised to stay a month, Alcott remained in Dedham for seven weeks. The pleas of the old man and young woman that she remain to ease their loneliness tore at her heart. At last she could bear this misery no longer and gave final notice. As she said her farewells, the young woman pressed a small purse into Alcott's hands. She did not open it until she stood at the side of the windy highroad, waiting for the stagecoach. Dreaming of the wages she could bring home to her family, Alcott found four dollars. Four dollars for seven weeks of backbreaking and demeaning toil! It was an outrage almost greater than she could endure. There seemed only one fitting response to the insult: When she reached home, she returned the four dollars by mail.

Alcott returned to find her family, as usual, barely keeping poverty at bay. In Concord, the writer Nathaniel Hawthorne, a family friend, purchased Hillside. Alcott's dream of returning to her beloved sanctuary was swept away.

Nathaniel Hawthorne, renowned American author and family friend of the Alcotts. His novel The Blithedale Romance *was based upon a transcendentalist commune similar to Fruitlands.*

Money from the sale enabled the Alcotts to rent a somewhat more comfortable house on Pinckney Street in Beacon Hill. Abba Alcott had pressed herself to the limit for several years, caring for as many immigrants as she could and trying to earn a living. At times, Louisa Alcott wrote of the burdens placed on her mother's—and her own—shoulders. "Father idle," she noted grimly in her diary. As for her youngest sister, the much-petted May (model for Amy in *Little Women*), the young writer observed testily, "She is doing nothing but growing." She often wondered if this scrambling to put food on the table and keep a roof overhead would ever cease.

Alcott took in laundry for two dollars a week; she sewed mountains of sheets, as many as a dozen a day, for whatever pay she could make. Her mother went off to her work, and her youngest sister attended school. Lizzie Alcott served as housekeeper—"our angel in a cellar kitchen," as Alcott called her. Bronson Alcott recorded his thoughts endlessly in his journals and discussed ideas with his circle of companions. Anna and Louisa Alcott also established a school in the parlor. Although they found the work of correcting slates and reciting the alphabet tedious, there was little else they could do. For young women of their class, teaching was virtually the only kind of work considered respectable. And to some, the fact that a young girl had to work at all seemed undignified.

The most exciting event of Alcott's year was the publication, in September 1852, of her first poem. She became a published writer when "Sunlight," appearing under the name Flora Fairfield, appeared in *Peterson's*, the nation's largest women's magazine. Alcott received payment for her effort and began to envision herself as a famous author.

To outsiders, Alcott, tall and grave, with a great cloud of chestnut hair, seemed serious and self-contained—no one could have known what dreams and ceaseless curiosity she carried inside. A visitor to the family at that time noticed her "earnest face, dark eyes" and sensed that there was something special about Alcott, about "her expressions of profound interest in other things than those which usually occupy the thoughts of young ladies." She did not have time to think about the latest fashions, much as she may have longed for silk dresses, cashmere shawls, and hair ribbons of her own. For all the year's labors, Alcott's teaching and sewing earned her $105 in 1852.

If her writing was to be the salvation of the family, Alcott determined to try her hand at different sorts of stories. She wanted to transform her miserable experience at Dedham into a salable account. With every high hope, Alcott

Hawthorne often retired to his study in the pines when in need of peace and quiet. Like Alcott, he felt most able to write during moments of solitude.

Time-consuming typesetting and binding methods made printing books in the 19th century a laborious task. Alcott's works were made available to the public through a printing office much like the one pictured above.

approached James Fields, Boston's most eminent publisher, with her manuscript. His most recent success had been the publication of Nathaniel Hawthorne's *The Scarlet Letter*. From his desk in an office above the Old Corner Bookstore in the heart of old Boston, he decided which authors' manuscripts to publish. He rejected Alcott's story out of hand. "Stick to your teaching, Miss Alcott," he told her flatly. "You can't write." Her heart

pounding, Alcott clutched her manuscript and fled.

Alcott, with her streak of stubbornness and an innate sense of her own talent, was too stouthearted to be discouraged for long. She stored away the "Out to Service" story and, still determined to make another submission to James Fields one day, continued writing. Her faith in herself soon brought results: As Flora Fairfield, she sold "The Rival Prima Donnas," a lurid tale of love and treachery set in the world of theater, to the *Saturday Evening Gazette*. Editors would indeed read her stories—and she had $10 from one of the nation's largest weeklies to prove it.

Only a few weeks later, in time for her to slip a slim volume into her mother's Christmas stocking, Alcott's first book appeared. *Flower Fables*, stories and poems she had once told to one of Emerson's small daughters on long afternoons in the Alcotts' barn, appeared in an edition of 1,600. The publication of these stories did not make Alcott a famous writer—much less a rich one—overnight. Still, "My book came out," she recorded in her journal, "and people began to think topsey-turvy Louisa would amount to something after all." Although *Fables* added only $32 to her fortunes, she knew that it was the first of what would be many successes.

Abba Alcott realized that her daughter's imagination deserved nurturing. She fitted up a third-floor room for her daughter, and there the writer retreated from the family's commotion and cares. "I am in my garret with my paper round me, and a pile of apples to eat while I write my journal, plan stories, and enjoy the patter of rain on the roof, in peace and quiet." Alcott

Alcott's own personality was the model for Jo March, the rebellious, warmhearted tomboy protagonist of Little Women. *The family poet, Jo often retired to the privacy of her own room in order to write and dream of the future.*

would later re-create this garret in *Little Women*, as the hideaway where Jo March retreated to find her writer's voice and to create the stories she held close to her heart.

Alcott poses with a book. Throughout her life, the author would be torn between the desire to take care of her family and the need to be independent.

FIVE

Partings

In 1855, Abba Alcott began to weary of her grueling working life, and the restless Alcotts continued to long for life in the country. When a relative offered them a rent-free house in Walpole, New Hampshire, they packed off for the town set in hills near the Massachusetts border. "Here Father can have a garden, Mother can rest, and Anna and I can go from here to our teaching, wherever it may be," Alcott wrote. Her sister was 24, and she was 22. They both longed to be off on their own, where they could help contribute to the family's welfare. Anna Alcott set off to teach in Syracuse, and Louisa Alcott returned to Boston—"to seek my fortune," as she put it.

With a trunk of dresses she had stitched herself, $20 that she had earned for stories that appeared in the *Gazette*, and a stack of manuscripts that she intended to sell, Louisa Alcott moved into a boardinghouse with her hopes as her close companions. Editors at the *Gazette* were eager to buy her stories, and more and more of them appeared in print. She treasured the time on her own and the chance to be independent from her family. Even so, her thoughts were always given over to their welfare, and soon she found herself longing to see everyone in Walpole.

The family, as usual, needed every penny Alcott could send home. Propelled by their need, one night she found herself sewing until dawn, making a "dozen pillow cases, one dozen sheets, six fine cambric neckties, and two dozen handkerchiefs," for which she received four dollars. Hard as she

In 1856 Lizzie Alcott, considered the beauty of the family, contracted scarlet fever. Her protracted illness and death constituted one of the greatest sorrows of Louisa Alcott's life.

and fixed it nicely," Alcott wrote. "Her old one had haunted me all winter, and I want her to look neat. She is so graceful and pretty and loves beauty so much, it is hard for her to be poor and wear other people's ugly things. You and I have learned not to mind *much*; but when I think of her I long to dash out and buy the finest hat the limited sum of ten dollars can procure." For her father, Alcott meant to buy "new neckties and some paper" so that "he can keep on with the beloved diaries though the heavens fall," and for Lizzie, "who is wearing all the old gowns. . . . a new one." Her dream was to save her family from their cramped and needy existence—as for her youngest sister, Alcott hoped one day to see "the dear child in silk and lace, with plenty of pictures and 'bottles of cream,' Europe, and all she longs for."

Alcott's dreams soon gave way to very troubling worries. In the summer of 1856, her sister Lizzie contracted scarlet fever from a family that her mother was nursing. Her case was very serious. When Alcott returned to Walpole for the summer, she was shocked to find her sister, frail and quiet from the start, ravaged by the disease. The family physician predicted she would recover, but Alcott felt herself weighed down by fear. In fact, a terrible family drama was unfolding.

Lizzie Alcott continued to grow weaker over the course of a year. The

worked, she reserved little that she earned for herself. "I am grubbing away as usual," Alcott wrote to her sister Anna, "trying to get money enough to buy Mother a nice warm shawl. I have eleven dollars, all my own earnings,—five for a story, and four for the pile of sewing I did. . . ." Although the older Alcott sisters longed for stylish dresses, they put sister May's wishes before their own: "I got a crimson ribbon for a bonnet for May, and I took my straw following summer, doctors advised sea air, and Abba Alcott took her daughter to the seashore north of Boston. Her journal records the progress of the disease: Although she took her daughter out for drives in the sea air and baths in the ocean, her condition worsened. Lizzie was, she reported, "thinner than ever and looks the incarnation of frailty. Her smile is sweet but ghastly—at times she is dreadfully distressed."

Bronson Alcott felt that a return to Concord, with its atmosphere of serenity and its community of old friends, might be helpful to his ailing daughter. Because Bronson also missed the intellectual companionship of Emerson and Thoreau, he decided to return to the village. Once again, Emerson helped the family to buy a dilapidated old homestead—the family would call it Orchard House—and the Alcotts brought Lizzie home.

The family moved into temporary lodgings as they waited for Orchard House to be repaired. Lizzie grew weaker and weaker. By the coming of the new year, 1858, the Alcotts knew the truth. "Lizzie much worse," Louisa Alcott acknowledged that January. "Dr. G. says there is no hope. A hard thing to bear; but if she is only to suffer, I pray she may go soon.... Anna took the house-keeping; so Mother and I could devote ourselves to her. Sad, quiet days in her room, and strange

Through the character of delicate, patient Beth in Little Women, *Alcott brought her much-loved sister back to life. The whole world would eventually know of her sister's quiet bravery.*

The purchase of Orchard House enabled the Alcotts to return to Concord. Lizzie Alcott's illness, however, prevented the long-awaited homecoming from being a happy one.

nights keeping up the fire and watching the dear little shadow try to while away the long sleepless hours without troubling me. She sews, reads, sings softly, and lies looking at the fire,—so sweet and patient and so worn, my heart is broken to see the change." It was the sickroom and the night watch Alcott would re-create in *Little Women*, as Jo waits through the long winter nights at her sister's side. Lizzie, wasted by disease and nearly bald, had come to look like a woman twice her age: "What she suffered was seen in the face," Alcott wrote, "for at twenty-three she looked like a woman of forty, so worn was she."

Early in March, Lizzie put down her needle, saying that she found it "too heavy." She said her farewells by giving away her favorite possessions. To Anna, she gave her desk; she bequeathed her letters and favorite books to the rest of the family. On March 14, with the family gathered round, she lost consciousness and breathed her last. "So the first break comes," mourned Alcott in her journal. "I know what death means,—a liberator for her, a teacher for us." Lizzie's suffering had been almost more than Alcott could bear. Grief stricken though she was, she felt relief at the end of her sister's helpless suffering: "I am glad to know she is safe from pain and age in some world where her innocent soul must be happy."

Beth and Jo. Like Jo March, Alcott had to support others despite her personal sorrows. Though still grief stricken by her sister's death, she moved to Boston and began earning money for the family.

Marmee, based upon Abba Alcott, tends to Beth in her illness. Though no one could have wished for a better mother than Marmee, Alcott always claimed that the character's many virtues paled before those of her own mother.

The first wedding in Alcott's own family was that of her sister Anna to John Pratt. Though happy for the couple, Alcott could not help but feel saddened by Anna's departure from the Alcott home.

Eventually, Alcott would give expression to her anguish in another way. As she re-created the character of Lizzie in her portrayal of Beth in *Little Women*, Alcott was able to convey her sister's bravery and grace in the face of so much pain. When the book appeared, the world would know of Lizzie's goodness, as well as the grief that enveloped the Alcotts.

A few weeks after Lizzie's death, Anna brought news that would change the Alcott family still more. She announced her engagement to John Pratt, the son of another Concord family. The family approved of John—he was an even-tempered and generous young man—although Louisa Alcott, romantic as she was, probably found the earnest young clerk a bit dull. Louisa Alcott and her mother both found the prospect of losing Anna extremely painful: Abba Alcott wanted to keep her daughters forever at her side, especially since she had lost Lizzie. "We have forgotten," Abba observed in her journal, "that she is her own for any destiny that she pursues." Louisa Alcott, too, turned to her diary to express her grief: "I moaned in private over my great loss, and said I'd never forgive J. for taking Anna from me; but I shall if he makes her happy."

Anna Pratt would remain close to her family, living nearby and returning to visit as often as possible. Nevertheless, she had wearied of the tensions

Beth March in a moment of contemplation. Knowing she has little time left to live, she sheds a secret tear at the sight of a healthy, happy boy passing by on the street.

that plagued the household centered around her father and looked to marriage as an escape from that situation: "In a household like my father's where poverty and trial and disappointment have continually been trying the tempers and hearts, very quick tempers, very warm hearts, there has necessarily been much disquiet, and great

Jo March writes avidly in her garret. Even though financial considerations forced Alcott to take any odd job that came her way, she found enough time to write short stories and, eventually, novels.

clashing of wills and though we have always loved and dearly labored for each other, there has been a want of that harmony which is the great charm of family life."

Anna's perspective differed from that of Louisa, who keenly felt the need to take care of her parents. Yet Anna was free to make her own life only because her sister Louisa had taken on the responsibility of maintaining the Alcotts. "The old people need an abiding place," Louisa Alcott mused. "And now that death and love have taken

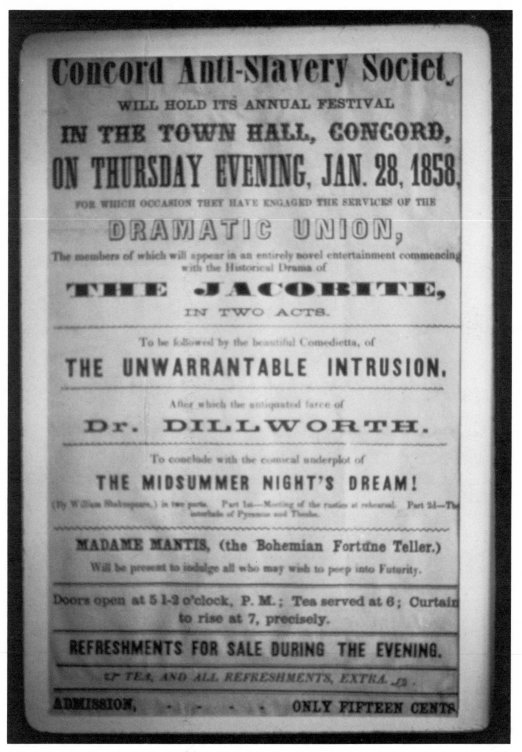

Alcott and her sisters were members of Concord's local theatrical group, which on at least one occasion raised funds to support the abolitionist movement.

two of us away, I can, I hope, soon manage to care for the remaining four."

In October Alcott returned to Boston, mourning Lizzie's death, restless, and in search of work. She was haunted by images of her sister's suffering—the long months of Lizzie's dying had left Alcott feeling almost as if she could not go on. She scoured Boston for work, recognizing that she was the family's "only breadwinner," but could find nothing. One afternoon, as she walked along the Mill Dam on the outskirts of Boston, her troubles seemed to gather force and overwhelm her. The thought of leaping from the dam into the Charles River crept into her mind. Somehow she was able to pull herself away from the brink of despair. "It seemed so cowardly to run away before the battle was over. I couldn't do it."

Undaunted as ever, Alcott surveyed her prospects. "So I said firmly, there *is* work for me, and I'll have it, and went home resolved to take fate by the throat and shake a living out of her." She was about to take a grim assignment—sewing for 10 hours a day for 30

A cartoon depicting the case of Henry Brown, a slave who was shipped to Philadelphia and set free by northern abolitionists. Before the Civil War, concerned citizens from both the North and South formed the Underground Railroad to help slaves escape.

girls at a reform school—when a position as governess was offered her. Alcott accepted eagerly and went back to writing in yet another peaceful garret room.

Alcott returned to Concord for her sister's wedding on the morning of May 23, 1860, the anniversary of her parents' wedding in Boston 30 years before. Louisa Alcott was a bridesmaid; Anna, wearing a gray silk dress and lilies of the valley in her hair, was married in the parlor of Orchard House by Sam May, her maternal uncle. Afterward, the guests, who included Emerson and Thoreau, feasted on cake and wine and danced under the great elm on the lawn.

Alcott recorded the event in her diary, but not without expressing her grief: "I mourn the loss of my Nan, and am not comforted." Of the lively household of four daughters, now only she and May remained.

Anna's departure left Abba Alcott feeling bereft, and so Louisa soon moved back into Concord as her mother's companion. She was writing *Moods*, the novel that she would publish in 1864. Never had she lived a book so completely: "I wrote all day," Alcott recalled, "and planned nearly all night, being quite possessed by my work. I was perfectly happy, and seemed to have no wants." After several months' work, she reported that she "finished the book, or a rough draft of it, and put it away to settle."

Moods, the story of Sylvia Yule, a young woman who must choose between two men who love her, contains a character strongly modeled after Henry Thoreau. Since her childhood days, when Thoreau had made of all the country surrounding Concord a classroom, Alcott had admired him. Reticent and eccentric as he sometimes appeared, and severe and withdrawn as people often found him, Alcott felt that she knew the real Thoreau—one who communed with every creature of field and stream and who fearlessly sheltered runaway slaves making their way to Canada on the Underground Railroad (a secret network of individuals who ran stations providing food and shelter to the fugitives). In her description of the alluring Adam Warwick, protagonist of *Moods*, Alcott's feelings for Thoreau come to life: He is "broad-shouldered, strong-limbed and browned by wind and weather. A massive head, covered by waves of ruddy brown hair, gray eyes that seemed to pierce through all disguises, an eminent nose, and beard.... Power, intellect and courage were stamped on face and figure." Since her adolescence, Alcott had seen in Thoreau a man she could admire and love. But because he was bound up so completely with his own writing, there was little Alcott could do to win his heart.

In the two years following Anna's marriage, Thoreau's health began to fail. He was suffering from the most common 19th-century killer, tuberculosis. By the spring of 1862, he was too weak to enjoy his beloved countryside. Abba Alcott gathered herbs and con-cocted her own special remedies, but to no avail. From his bed in his mother's farmhouse in Concord, he calmly put his affairs in order. His greatest concern was that his sister Sophia should look after his precious journals and notebooks. He died on May 6, and Alcott felt the loss keenly.

The Champs Élysées in Paris. The success of Hospital Sketches *and* Moods *left Alcott with time to fulfill her youthful dream of seeing Europe. She traveled as a paid companion through England, Germany, France, and Switzerland.*

SIX

Little Women

Much as she grieved for Lizzie and Thoreau, Alcott managed to turn her sadness to activity and her brooding to the act of writing. Later that year, when she volunteered as a Civil War nurse, those close to her thought it typical of her that she chose to focus her energies on useful work. People in Concord, who knew of her strenuous efforts to provide for the Alcotts, were not surprised to learn that in Washington she had worked until she dropped from fever.

As she began to recover her strength and was able to enjoy the success of *Hospital Sketches* and *Moods*, Alcott decided to fulfill one of her own cherished dreams. Since girlhood she had longed to see Europe. As her earnings from writing were still meager, though, she signed on as a paid companion to a young invalid woman and set sail in July 1865. Traveling to England, Germany, France, and Switzerland satisfied her taste for new scenery and cultures. Alcott was, as ever, impetuous and eager to explore her surroundings. She chafed under the demands of her charge and returned from the journey earlier than she had planned.

Though she had made same money publishing romances and thrillers before the war, Alcott wanted to write more serious fiction. The success of *Hospital Sketches* and *Moods* had encouraged her, and she decided to explore different ways of writing. Alcott immediately set to work at her desk. The family had run up debts in her absence, and she intended to write her way out of their difficulties. Alcott wrote rapidly, with all the energy she

The first edition of Little Women, *illustrated by Alcott's sister May, sold out almost immediately. When demand for the book increased in the United States and orders poured in from abroad, Alcott was asked to write a sequel.*

given much thought to writing for children, although at this time she had begun writing stories for a children's magazine, *Merry's Museum*, and served as one of its editors. She was not at all sure that she could succeed with *Little Women*.

Yet she was willing to try her hand. "Marmee, Anna and May all approve my plan," Alcott noted in the spring of 1868. Still, she had her doubts about this undertaking: "So I plod away, though I don't enjoy this sort of thing: Never liked girls or knew many, except my sisters; but our plays and experiences may prove interesting, though I doubt it."

Her heart and mind were not totally given over to this project. She did not write in a state of creative abandon, as she had during the composition of *Moods*. Still, she produced her work steadily and very quickly, and *Little Women* soon took shape. Her memories gave the book its form. As chapter after chapter spilled from her pen, she reinvented the Alcotts. The family closeness, laughter, and good times that she had cherished at Hillside lay at the center of *Little Women*. As Alcott described the life and times of the four March sisters—Anna as tranquil Meg, herself as aspiring writer Jo, Lizzie as fragile Beth, and May as willful Amy— she willed away all the distress that had accompanied her family's poverty. What remained were the abiding ties

could muster. Soon she found herself attempting a new kind of writing, a curious experiment that would become *Little Women*. She noted in her journal that her publisher, Thomas Niles, "wants a girls' story." Until this moment in her career, Alcott had not

When Alcott's publisher requested that she write a story for girls, her first reaction was negative. She had never written anything for children and as a tomboy had taken little interest in activities considered proper for girls.

A painting by May Alcott. May was the prototype for the temperamental Amy March, who went to Europe to develop her artistic talents. May, in fact, eventually did go abroad to study art.

that Alcott often had wished for in her own family—but was able to create completely only in her fiction.

She revised scarcely a word as she sat at her small writing table day after day. In a way, the story seemed to tell itself, for Alcott was, in some senses, transcribing her memories. She was also creating a new kind of literature for children—a story that was neither preachy nor sentimental, but a faithful account of four sisters as they actually lived and spoke.

The world of *Little Women* centers around the March family hearthside, where Marmee and her daughters gather in the evenings, needlework at hand, to share the day's events. Into this circle of warmth and companionship they admit Laurie, the lonely and motherless boy next door, who will one day lose his heart to Jo. He is drawn to the four sisters' lightheartedness and to their kindness and bustling activity. Jo, Beth, Meg, and Amy strive to overcome their own faults, just as the characters in *Pilgrim's Progress*, their father's favorite book, seek after their own best selves. In the year of Reverend March's absence as a Civil War chaplain, his daughters pass from childhood to adolescence on their way to becoming independent and generous "little women."

At last, having scarcely left her room for two and a half months, Alcott put down her pen. She had finished *Little Women* and sent off more than 200 pages to her publisher. The book had sapped her energies: "Very tired, head full of pain from over-work," she wrote. Her relief at having completed her "book for girls" was clouded by worry for her mother. "Heart heavy about Marmee, who is growing feeble." Abba Alcott's health was failing, and it seemed to Louisa Alcott almost as if her mother had turned into an old woman overnight.

The book arrived in time for Abba Alcott's 68th birthday. Bound in brown with gilt lettering, *Little Women: Meg, Jo, Beth and Amy, the Story of Their Lives, A Girls' Book* appeared on September 30, 1868. It seemed appropriate that this was an "all-Alcott" production, with illustrations by artist-sister May. Alcott fretted about the book's reception—would her readers find the simple story to be dull? "Not a bit sensational, but simple and true, for we really lived most of it" was Alcott's assessment of her creation. "If it is successful," she mused, "that will be the reason for it." It was soon apparent that she had worried needlessly: 2,000 copies sold out almost immediately.

Little Women began to sell abroad as well. Within a month, Alcott was able to report, "Saw Mr. N. from Roberts Brothers, and he gave me good news of the book. An order from London for an edition came in: First-edition gone and more called for. Expects to see three or four thousand before the New Year." Her publisher was so encouraged that he asked Alcott to produce a second part for *Little Women* as quickly as possible. "A little success is so inspiring," she exulted. She felt that she could dash off the second volume devoted to the Marches. "I can do a chapter a day," she vowed, "and in a month I mean to be done."

Concord felt confining after months of hard work there, so Alcott went off to a rented room in Boston. The peace

Mr. Bhaer dresses a wound as his wife, Jo, looks on. The second volume of Little Women, *in which all of the March girls married, was an enormous bestseller and at the time made Alcott the most famous author in America.*

and quiet and the absence of Alcotts suited her. Alcott wrote furiously, her pen scratching away on her favorite blue-lined paper. The pages mounted up, and she was amazed at her own

"Louise Alcott"
The Children's Friend.

Lizbeth B. Comins

*Alcott reads to a group of children.
Childless herself, the author thought of
her books as offspring.*

productivity. "I have," she noted wryly, "written like a steam engine." She was scarcely eating or sleeping and spent her 36th birthday without a visit from her family. "Alone, writing hard" was her entry for November 29, 1868.

In the second volume of *Little Women*, Alcott explored the young adulthood of her characters. She enjoyed this excursion into the future, where, she felt, "my fancy has more play." As Alcott wrote, great changes overtook the March household. Part two opens three years after the conclusion of part one. Meg married John, and Alcott re-created her sister's simple wedding for her readers. Jo, as usual, chose her own independent ways, giving her hand to the bookish, kindly Professor Bhaer—not to Laurie, though her young readers had pleaded for the match. Beth's illness consumed the March household and left readers everywhere weeping at the loss. And Amy went off to pursue dreams in Europe, where she developed her talent as an artist and accepted Laurie's proposal as they rowed together across a lake in Switzerland.

The success of the second volume was nothing short of extraordinary. Readers everywhere were waiting ea-

Amy March accepts Laurie's proposal of marriage. Their betrothal came as a surprise to the readers of the sequel to Little Women, *who expected Laurie to marry Jo instead.*

gerly to follow the fortunes of Jo, Beth, Meg, and Amy. The book appeared on April 14, 1869. Within two weeks it was clear that Alcott's creation would be a runaway best-seller. Thirteen thousand copies sold out almost immediately. *Little Women* appeared in every bookseller's window, and all of America was laughing and crying over the simple tale of the Marches. Almost overnight, Louisa May Alcott was the most famous author in America.

Reporters lay in wait around Or-

chard House, hoping for a glimpse of *Little Women*'s creator. Alcott dreaded this kind of publicity. "People begin to come and stare at the Alcotts," she fumed into her journal. All the fuss made her want to "dodge into the woods" as her neighbor Nathaniel Hawthorne had done when his novels made him famous. Bronson Alcott, on the other hand, enjoyed the commotion. For once he gave his whole-hearted approval to his headstrong second daughter: "It is an honor not anticipated for a daughter of mine to have won so wide a celebrity, and a greater honor that she takes this so modestly, unwilling to believe there is not something unreal in it all."

Louisa Alcott did accede to her readers' wishes in one important way. Letters had poured in from girls across the country, pleading that the March girls be married in the second volume. The author's feelings about this were complex. "Girls write to ask who the little women will marry," Alcott observed, "as if that was the only end of a woman's life." She did give way to the clamoring for husbands—but she still wanted to write about other possibilities in women's lives.

Soon after completing *Little Women*, she wrote a series of sketches about unmarried women for young girls. Her subjects were one and all accomplished—doctors, teachers, writers— and she titled her essays "Happy Women." "Liberty," she reminded her readers, "is a better husband than love to many of us." Nevertheless, as Alcott compared her life to Anna's, who had a husband and two little boys, she sometimes felt wistful. "I sell *my* children," Alcott wrote of her creations, "and though they feed me, they don't love me as [Anna's] do."

Even so, Alcott ended the year 1869—a year of triumph— feeling a measure of security and happiness. A new mass audience for inexpensive books—young people between the ages of 12 and 16—had developed, and royalties from *Little Women* came flooding in. Alcott was able to write her publishers with "many thanks for the check which made my Christmas an unusually merry one." The years of struggle had passed, and she sharply felt that relief. "After toiling so many years along the uphill road—always a hard one for women writers—it is grateful to me to find the way growing easier at last."

Portrait of Alcott reading a letter. The success of her books, though exhilarating, left Alcott exhausted. As she grew older, the symptoms of the mercury poisoning that she contracted during the Civil War began to plague her with unnerving frequency.

SEVEN

Travels and Triumphs

Alcott's two years of intensive work on *Little Women* left her ecstatic at her own successes. Even so, she felt quite spent. The symptoms of her old Civil War illness reappeared: She was plagued by "aches, cough, and weariness" and entered the complaint "feel quite used up" in her journal.

A journey to Europe, this time in a state of luxury befitting a famous author, seemed the answer to Alcott's difficulties. Alcott and her sister May planned their travels together: For more than a year they would take in the sights in France, Italy, and England. May, who delighted in every new vista, proved a lively traveling companion. Alcott, admired and pampered wherever she traveled, for once found herself amused by her celebrity status.

Nevertheless, it was clear that Alcott's health was failing. When she and May settled into lodgings in Brittany, the writer took to her bed. A British physician residing at their pension instantly recognized Alcott's symptoms: mercury poisoning associated with the calomel used to treat typhoid fever. She was troubled especially by tormenting pains in her legs and a continually aching head. In a letter home, Alcott explained what she had learned about the poisoning: "The mercury lies round in a body ... till a weak spot appears; then it goes there and makes trouble. I don't know anything about it, only the leg is the curse of my life." Her doctor advised a regimen that seemed to help a bit: draughts of wine to promote circulation, long woolen underwear to keep warm, doses of iodine

Town of Quimper, France. Alcott's second journey to Europe, this time as a famous author, was far more luxurious than her first. Wherever she and her sister May went, they were greeted by crowds of admiring readers.

or potash as an antidote. Alcott detailed her treatment in letters to the family. Anna's husband, John Pratt, had also received calomel when he served in the Civil War, and his symptoms closely resembled Alcott's. Neither Pratt nor Alcott would find any real remedy for the devastating effects of the poison.

The sisters moved on to Rome, taking lodgings there for the winter. May Alcott eagerly applied herself to her beloved drawing lessons and explored the city. Alcott felt ill a good deal of the time and kept to the apartment. By now, she was taking morphine to help her sleep. Cheering news did arrive from her publisher. *Little Women* had sold 60,000 copies, and *An Old Fashioned Girl*, the novel Alcott had sent to press as she embarked for Europe, had sold 36,000.

The winter in Rome brought sad tidings as well. John Pratt's condition had deteriorated quickly. He died on Alcott's 38th birthday, November 29, 1870. Alcott was grief stricken at the loss of the steadfast, good-natured brother-in-law who served as the model for John Brooke, Meg's husband, in *Little Women*. "No born brother was ever dearer," she wrote to Anna, "and each year I loved and respected and admired him more and more."

She was also concerned for the welfare of her sister and two nephews. As

LOUISA M. ALCOTT'S FAMOUS BOOKS.

AN OLD-FASHIONED GIRL.
PRICE $1.50.
ROBERTS BROTHERS, *Publishers, Boston.*

Alcott sent the manuscript for An Old Fashioned Girl *to her publisher just before embarking for Europe. During her stay in Rome, she learned that the book had sold 36,000 copies.*

usual, Alcott translated worry into work. "Began to write a new book, 'Little Men,' that John's death may not leave A. and the dear little boys in want

John Sewall Pratt. As long as she lived, Alcott provided generously for her nephews.

... in writing and thinking of the dear little lads, to whom I must be a father now, I found comfort for my sorrow."

Anna's tragedy caused Alcott to long for home. Although she called the year in Rome "very pleasant in spite of constant pain. . . . and home anxieties," she was weary and longing for familiar faces. May stayed behind to study drawing in London. Alcott arrived in Boston Harbor in June where Bronson Alcott and her publisher, Thomas Niles, welcomed her at the dock bearing a red banner emblazoned with the title of her latest creation, *Little Men: Life at Plumfield with Jo's Boys*.

Abba Alcott had aged considerably in her daughter's absence: Alcott was quite disturbed by the change in her mother. Abba, model for beloved Marmee in *Little Women*—the mother who struggled to tame Jo's temper—was no longer strong enough to comfort or care for her children. As Alcott sketched her mother's condition in her journal, she sounded the themes of the next years of her life: "Mother feeble and much aged by this year of troubles. I shall never go far away from her again."

Responsible as Alcott felt for her family's welfare, she needed time to herself and distance from their consuming demands. Over the next two years or so, she shuttled back and forth between Concord and Boston. Alcott kept a city retreat for herself

Frederick (pictured) *and John Pratt were left to the care of Alcott and their mother Anna upon their father's death. Alcott, the family's only source of income, considered herself a type of father for the boys.*

where she could rest and write. All her novels had proved so successful that she could well have given up working altogether. Yet writing had become a way of life for her, and one story, as Jo March might have said, *would* follow the other. "I try to get well so that I may work," she wrote. "Anything is better than the invalidism I hate worse than death."

Though she was renowned as an author of children's books, Alcott intended to write at least one more novel for adults. The experience of her own young womanhood and the very limited opportunities to use her intelligence in meaningful work continued to preoccupy her. Tucked away in a trunk of manuscripts, one story, "Success," an autobiographical account of her attempts to make an independent living, seemed very much worth the telling. When one publisher asked Alcott for a long story that could be serialized in a magazine, she dusted off "Success."

Deciding she would call the novel *Work*, she plunged into writing. "Can't work slowly," she noted in her journal, "the thing possesses me, and I must obey till it's done." Alcott drew many threads of her life into *Work*, including her days as a struggling and impoverished working girl, her servitude in Dedham, and her memories of the Civil War. Christie, the novel's central character, is very much Alcott's alter

While in Rome, Alcott received word that Little Women *had sold 60,000 copies. Word of Pratt's death from mercury poisoning, however, cast a pall over the good news.*

Alcott was greeted upon her arrival from Europe in Boston Harbor by her father and Thomas Niles, her publisher. The two men carried a banner inscribed with the title of her newest work, Little Men.

ego. She is quick-witted, observant, energetic—and pressed into all sorts of difficult and demeaning work.

Like Alcott, Christie tries her hand as servant, governess, and paid companion. Overworked and miserably ill paid, her intelligence is dismissed and her abilities are ignored. Although Christie does marry (her husband, the gentle, introspective David Sterling, is another character modeled after Thoreau), she soon loses her husband in the Civil War. Christie does not marry again, but makes her own way and supports her child. She devises her own solution to her plight, finds work of her choosing, and helps other young women find work as well.

LITTLE MEN:

LIFE AT PLUMFIELD WITH JO'S BOYS.

BY

LOUISA M. ALCOTT,

AUTHOR OF "LITTLE WOMEN," "AN OLD-FASHIONED GIRL," "EIGHT
COUSINS," "ROSE IN BLOOM," "UNDER THE LILACS," "JACK
AND JILL," "HOSPITAL SKETCHES," "WORK," "SILVER
PITCHERS," "AUNT JO'S SCRAP-BAG."

With Illustrations.

QUI LEGIT REGIT

BOSTON:
ROBERTS BROTHERS.
1883.

*Filled with grief over Pratt's death, Alcott immediately began
writing* Little Men. *She thought of the book as a way to secure
the financial futures of her widowed sister and two nephews.*

Lucy Stone, a well-known social reformer, edited The Woman's Journal, *one of the first women's-rights publications. Her friend Alcott wrote numerous articles for the magazine.*

thing she had lately turned her hand to, it was an enormous success.

Alcott maintained a keen interest in the accomplishments of working women. Her experience at the Union Hotel Hospital made her especially anxious that more women enter medicine. One of her Boston cousins, Lucy Sewall, became one of the country's first female physicians. Lucy had delivered Anna's second son, John, and Alcott followed her career avidly.

Alcott also worked actively on behalf of women's suffrage, an ongoing struggle to win voting rights for women. Although the suffragists' proposals were first introduced in 1848, women were not granted the right to vote on a nationwide basis until 1920. Alcott contributed countless articles to *The Woman's Journal*, a women's rights newspaper edited by her friend Lucy Stone, a leading social reformer of the period who campaigned for the abolition of slavery as well as for suffrage and other women's rights. In 1879, Alcott became the first woman in Concord to register for the vote in the village's school-committee election. She also traveled about the town in her carriage, canvassing from door to door and urging women to register for this election. The women she approached seemed to her "timid and slow." "So hard to move people out of the old ruts," she complained. "I haven't patience enough. If they won't see and

Work was published in 1873, the same year that Alcott had started working on it. As was the case with every-

Women voting at a municipal election in Boston. Alcott, an active participant in the woman suffrage movement, was the first woman to register for the vote in Concord's school-committee election.

work I let 'em alone and steam along my own way." She soon returned to writing for the *Journal* because she found personal contact trying.

In the eyes of many women, though, Alcott herself was the outstanding example of what a gifted, determined woman could do with her talents. Alcott discovered what an important symbol she had become when she attended the Women's Congress, a meeting of feminist activists held in Syracuse, New York, in 1875. As the speeches ended, masses of women and young girls thronged about her, squeezing her hand, asking for autographs, pleading with her to write more books. Characteristically, she was not pleased by the attention. "So this, this is fame," she grumbled. Still, as she pushed her way through the admiring crowd, Alcott, at the age of 43, began to understand how much she had inspired an entire generation of American women.

The Congress of Women meets at Madison Square Theatre. Much to her surprise, Alcott's hard-earned literary success made her a shining symbol of independence to the feminists of her time.

Bronson Alcott at home on the grounds of Orchard House. In his old age, he lectured extensively on philosophy and on the career of his famous daughter.

EIGHT

Tying the Thread

In her own reluctant yet responsible fashion, Alcott became the head of her family once her mother's energies began to fail. Bronson Alcott remained absorbed in his books and continued to lecture throughout the country on philosophical subjects. He also became known as "the grandfather of *Little Women*" and was often asked to speak about his famous daughter. Louisa Alcott provided for everyone, continued to work, and tried to evade the consequences of her own celebrity. "Reporters sit on the wall and take notes," she wrote from Concord. "Artists sketch me as I pick pears in my garden. . . . It looks like impertinent curiosity to me, but it is called 'fame,' and considered a blessing to be grateful for." Much as she might wish for it, she could never again retire into anonymity.

She gathered her family around her, satisfied at being able to care for them yet feeling somehow pensive and lonely. In 1874, Alcott took her mother, her sister, and her two nephews, Freddy and John, to Boston. Even as they set up housekeeping, she found herself musing on her dilemma. Happiness, she felt, was growing ever more elusive. "When I had youth, I had no money; now that I have the money, I have no time; and when I get the time, if ever I do, I shall have no health to enjoy life." Her spirits were at a low ebb: Alcott's sense of when her family's life left off and her own began remained curiously blurred.

May Alcott, however, had learned to live for her own talents and for herself. She returned from Europe to help nurse Abba Alcott, but she longed to pursue her career as a painter. Al-

LOUISA M. ALCOTT'S FAMOUS BOOKS.

ROSE IN BLOOM.

A SEQUEL TO
"EIGHT COUSINS."

Price $1.50.

ROBERTS BROTHERS, PUBLISHERS.

A Rose in Bloom *came out during a relatively peaceful period of Alcott's life. Though greatly pleased with the financial security she had won for her family, she sometimes felt weary of her role as the Alcott breadwinner.*

though Louisa Alcott did not allow herself to indulge many wishes, she encouraged those of her sister and soon sent May back to study in London and Paris. Because of her mother's

failing health and her own failure to find a suitable nurse in Boston, Alcott moved back to Concord with her mother and helped Anna to buy a house there. She confided her discontent only to her journal. "So she has *her* wish, and is happy," Alcott wrote after completing the house purchase. "When shall I have mine? Ought to be contented with knowing I help both sisters by my brains. But I'm selfish, and want to go away and rest in Europe. Never shall."

Alcott was of two minds, as always, about her situation. She did take pleasure in the security she had created for the Alcotts. Early in 1877, just after the appearance of her novel *Rose in Bloom*, she was able to report, "The year begins well. Nan keeps house; boys fine, tall lads . . . ; Father busy with his new book; Mother cosey with her sewing, letters." Much as she longed for the freedom May enjoyed, Alcott did take pride in her sister's accomplishments. "The money I invest in her pays the kind of interest I like," she observed. "She is so in earnest she will not stop for pleasure, rest, or society, but works away." Alcott believed in women who nurtured their own abilities. As May's career flourished, Alcott applauded her youngest sister's efforts to find her own way.

Once May had established a life in France, Abba Alcott waited anxiously for every letter. May's Parisian existence became her mother's beloved diversion. She sorely missed May's company, yet it was Louisa she wanted at her side. Throughout 1877, Abba grew more and more frail. On a rainy Sunday in November, four days before Louisa Alcott's 45th birthday, she peacefully breathed her last. Alcott was relieved that the suffering had ended but overcome with sorrow at the loss of her mother, Marmee. She once said that the character of *Little Women*'s Marmee was "all true, only not half good enough."

"I never wish her back," Alcott wrote, "but a great warmth seems gone out of my life, and there is no motive to go on now." The mother Alcott had longed to comfort, for whom she had written her way to riches, had endured a long and painful old age. Alcott's sense of self was tied very closely to the mother she so admired. When she lost Abba, it was as if she had lost a part of her very identity.

In the months after her mother's death, Alcott culled through her mother's letters and journals, all of them eloquent testaments to the life of the family, for Abba Alcott was herself a very fine writer. Bronson Alcott shared in this task and found that Abba's papers stirred many deep memories for him as well. His wife's descriptions vividly evoked the years of struggle: "I copy with tearful admiration these pages," he admitted, "and almost re-

pent now of my seeming incompetency, my utter inability to relieve the burdens laid upon her and my children during those years of helplessness." What he did not add was that the "years of helplessness" had ended only as a result of his daughter's labors.

The contrast between Louisa Alcott's life, given over to supporting her family, and May's grew more marked in the two years following Abba Alcott's death. In 1878, May married Ernest Nieriker, a prosperous Swiss-German banker, and settled into domestic happiness in Paris. She knew the Alcott household was submerged in grief, but even so, May could not apologize for the fact that she was happy: "Your letters seem almost a reproach to me for being able to forget that dear Marmee has gone from us even during this most happy time of my life." She simply refused to bend to the pressures to which Alcott acceded: "My future seems so full of beauty and joy I can think of nothing else. The lonely artistic life that once satisfied me seems the most dreary in the world."

The contrast was not lost on Alcott, who was torn between wishing her sister well and feeling heartsick that she had never known such happiness herself. "How different our lives are just now," she mused. "I so lonely, sad, and sick; she so happy, well, and blest. She always had the cream of things, and deserved it." Just as *Little Wom-*

In this 1868 letter to her mother, Alcott reports on the continuing success of her writing career. "I shall make my $1000 this year in spite of sickness and worry," she notes. Alcott used much of her income to support her family.

en's Amy, headstrong and petted, sought her own contentment, so did May. For Alcott, that approach to living seemed mysterious and unattainable.

On November 8, 1879, May gave birth to Louisa May Nieriker. News of the event ushered great joy into the Alcott household: "All doing well. Much rejoicing," Alcott wrote. "Nice little lass, and May very happy. Ah, if only I had been there! Too much happiness for me." It soon became clear that May's recovery was slow, and that her life was in danger. "May not doing well," read Alcott's journal entry early in December. "The weight on my heart is not at all imagination. . . . Hope it is my nerves; but this peculiar feeling has never misled me before." May died on December 29.

Her last wish was that the baby be sent to Alcott for safekeeping. Alcott could scarcely wait for the day when the child would be brought to Concord. The arrival of "Lulu" was what she came to live for. "May left me her little daughter for my own," Alcott wrote to a friend, "and if she comes over soon, I shall be too busy singing lullabies to one child to write tales for others."

When Lulu was nearly one, a governess and aunt, Sophie Nieriker, brought the child over from Europe. Lulu became the delight of Alcott's life. "She always comes to me," Alcott reported proudly, "and seems to have decided that I am really "Marmar." My heart is full of pride and joy, and the touch of the dear little hands seems to take away the bitterness of grief. I often go at night to see if she is really *here*, and the sight of the little head is sunshine to me." Lulu also brightened Bronson Alcott's life: Louisa Alcott smiled to see the two strolling in the garden.

Within several months of the child's arrival, Alcott was writing happily,

In 1885 Alcott moved her family into a spacious house on Louisburg Square in Boston. Within a few months, the stress of maintaining a household and caring for her ailing father was to take a fatal toll upon her always fragile health.

"Too busy to keep much of a journal. My life is absorbed in my baby." Christmas passed more happily in 1880, for Alcott was able to put aside sorrow. "A hard year for all," she mused, "but when I hold my Lulu I feel as if even death had its compensations. A new world for me."

Alcott applauded Lulu's every accomplishment and took comfort in the fact that the child reflected her lost mother's taste and temperament. "Her love of pictures is a passion," Alcott noted with satisfaction, "but she will not look at the common gay ones most babies enjoy. She chooses the delicate, well-drawn and painted figures.... over these she broods with rapture." Alcott saw May's spirit and temperament—headstrong and appreciative of beauty—reflected in her blond, blue-eyed niece.

Her absorption in Lulu caused Alcott to feel even greater impatience when her old illness struck again. The terrible headaches, the weariness, and pain in every muscle returned to plague her from time to time. "Wish I were stronger," she lamented, "so that I might take all the care of her. We seem to understand each other, but my nerves make me impatient, and noise wears upon me."

All in all, life in Concord went on serenely. But in the spring of 1882, the face of the village changed forever with Ralph Waldo Emerson's death. Alcott never forgot his enormous kindnesses to the family in times of desperate need or his invitation to her when she was an inquisitive girl who wanted to read every book in his library. "Our best and dearest American gone," she mourned. "The nearest and dearest friend Father has ever had, and the man who helped me most by his life, his books, his society. I can never tell all he has been to me." In Emerson, Alcott had found the kind of gentle encouragement that her father had not been able to give her. She always carried with her Emerson's appreciation of her talents.

In his old age, Bronson Alcott had himself grown gentler and more appreciative of his daughter's extraordinary gifts. He remained vigorous until he suffered a stroke late in 1882, at the age of 83. His vitality and will to live carried him through this crisis as well. His health began to mend, and though he never recovered completely, he continued to work for another six years. Anna Pratt and Louisa Alcott shared the burden of caring for their father.

Alcott's publisher, of course, continued to press her with requests for books and stories. She knew that her health was delicate, and she simply could not drive herself as she had before. The major work of her final period, completed over the course of several years, was *Jo's Boys*. In this

Bronson Alcott is best known today for the Transcendentalist philosophy he shared with Emerson. Though he could rarely provide for his family, he was much loved and respected by them.

novel, she carried Jo March into middle age and modeled Plumfield, the school Jo established with her husband, after the kind of ideal academy envisioned by her father.

Among her greatest pleasures at this time were her summer visits to Nonquit, a seaside village on the southern Massachusetts shore. There she spent relaxed and happy summers with Lulu at her side. The child was adventurous, as her aunt had been in long-ago Concord days. She waded straight into the waves, and Alcott found her namesake "very bold." Alcott bought her own cottage and settled in with her old cheer and energy: "Fixed my house, and enjoyed the rest and quiet immensely. Lulu wild with joy at the freedom."

In the fall of 1885, Louisa rented a house in Boston's elegant Louisburg Square for her entire family. It was an airy, spacious dwelling and everyone settled in happily: "Father . . . pleased with his new room; Lulu charmed with her big, sunny nursery and the playhouse left for her; boys in clover; and Nan ready for the new sort of housekeeping."

As usual, Alcott felt uncertain about

Alcott stands between her parents in front of the house in which she wrote Little Women. *The book earned Alcott a lasting place in the hearts of young readers.*

By the time she died at the age of 56, Louisa May Alcott was not only a respected author but an inspiration to women around the world.

the prospect of finding herself surrounded by her family. "I shall miss my quiet, carefree life . . . ," she admitted, "but it is best for all, so I shall try to bear the friction and the worry many persons always bring me."

Within months of the move, Alcott felt an onslaught of her old health troubles. "Another attack of vertigo . . . ill for a week; sleepless nights," she reported in September. "Head worked like a steam engine; would not stop. Planned 'Jo's Boys' to the end, and longed to get up and write it." As soon as she was able, she did seek relief in work, making good progress on *Jo's Boys*: "With much care about not overdoing, I had some pleasant hours when I forgot my body and lived in my mind."

As her condition worsened, so did her father's. The old man, at 85, was growing more and more feeble and helpless. His daughters mourned to see him so, and Alcott described his plight to a friend: "The still active mind beats against the prison bars, and rebels against the weakness of body that prevents the old independent life." The Alcott sisters both found it "so wearing to see this slow decline."

As 1887 passed, Alcott began to feel desperately ill. The large and boisterous household and the constant burden of Bronson Alcott's deterioration overwhelmed her. Rest and quiet seemed the only antidotes to the head-ache, pains, muscle tremors, hoarseness, indigestion, and sleeplessness that plagued her.

Hoping for recovery, she entered a special rest home supervised by her personal physician, Dr. Rhoda Lawrence. Alcott felt that careful attention, rest, and a regimen of special diet, massage, and soothing baths might restore her health. Anna and Lulu, who was now a lively, inquisitive seven-year-old, traveled out to Roxbury frequently to bring books, flowers, and reports of home. Much as Alcott missed everyone, she felt unable to bear the strains of the household.

She did seem, ever so slowly, to be healing. Early in the spring of 1888, the doctors pronounced her well enough to make an excursion into Louisburg Square. She visited her father, who was bedridden, weak, and aware that he was dying. Alcott knew this would most likely be their last visit.

On the way home, she leaned back against the carriage seat, complaining of a fearful headache. Within hours of her return to Roxbury, she lapsed into semiconsciousness. Her father died on March 4. Early in the morning of March 6, at the age of 56, America's beloved Louisa May Alcott passed from the earth. Readers around the world mourned the passing of the woman who created the timeless and vivid world of Jo, Beth, Meg, and Amy—four admirable *Little Women*.

FURTHER READING

Bedell, Madelon. *The Alcotts: The Biography of a Family*. New York: Potter, 1980.

Cheney, Ednah D. *Louisa May Alcott: Her Life, Letters and Journal*. New York: Chelsea House, 1980.

Elbert, Sarah. *A Hunger for Home: Louisa May Alcott and Little Women*. Philadelphia, PA: Temple University Press, 1984.

James, Edward T. (ed.) *Notable American Women 1607–1950: A Biographical Dictionary*. Cambridge, MA: Harvard University Press, 1974.

Kunitt, Stanley, and Howard Haycraft (eds.) *American Authors 1600–1900: A Biographical Dictionary of American Literature*. New York: Wilson, 1938.

Meigs, Cornelia. *Invincible Louisa*. Boston, MA: Little, Brown, 1933.

Robinson, Martha. *The Young Louisa May Alcott*. New York: Roy Publishers, 1963.

Saxton, Martha. *Louisa May*. Boston, MA: Houghton Mifflin, 1977.

Stern, Madeline B. *Louisa May Alcott*. Norman, OK: University of Oklahoma Press, 1950.

CHRONOLOGY

Nov. 29, 1832	Born Louisa May Alcott in Germantown, Pennsylvania
1834	Moves to Boston with family, where father, Bronson Alcott, opens his school
1840	Moves to Concord, Massachusetts, with family
1843	Moves with family to Fruitlands farmstead, established in Harvard, Massachusetts, by Bronson Alcott and friends
1845	Takes up residence with family at Hillside, in Concord
1849	Moves to Boston with family
1852	Publishes first poem, "Sunlight," in *Peterson's* magazine
1855	Publishes first book, *Flower Fables*
	Returns to Boston after family moves to Walpole, New Hampshire
1857	Returns to Concord with family; moves into Orchard House
1862	Travels to Washington, D.C., as volunteer Civil War nurse
1863	Becomes ill with typhoid fever
	Publishes *Hospital Sketches*
1864	Publishes *Moods*
1865	Embarks on first trip to Europe
1868	Publishes *Little Women*
1869	Completes second volume of *Little Women*
1870	Publishes an *Old Fashioned Girl*
1870–1871	Writes *Little Men;* travels to Europe with sister May
1873	Publishes novel *Work*
1874	Publishes *Eight Cousins*
1876	Publishes *Rose in Bloom*
1880	Brings orphaned niece, Louisa May Nieriker, to Boston
1885	Moves family to Louisburg Square, Boston
1886	Publishes *Jo's Boys*
March 6, 1888	Dies in Boston

INDEX

Kathleen Burke, an editor at *Smithsonian* magazine, writes frequently on historical subjects. She holds degrees from Wellesley College, Yale University, and Columbia University Graduate School of Journalism.

❖   ❖   ❖

Matina S. Horner is president of Radcliffe College and associate professor of psychology and social relations at Harvard University. She is best known for her studies of women's motivation, achievement, and personality development. Dr. Horner serves on several national boards and advisory councils, including those of the National Science Foundation, Time Inc., and the Women's Research and Education Institute. She earned her B. A. from Bryn Mawr College and Ph.D. from the University of Michigan, and holds honorary degrees from many colleges and universities, including Mount Holyoke, Smith, Tufts, and the University of Pennsylvania.